Heirloom

Dover Pocke...

CROSS-STITCH FLOWERS

☑ Classic patterns
☑ Checklists ☑ Space for notes

Features 26 simple designs

Gerda Bengtsson

Dover Publications, Garden City, New York

Copyright © 2025 by Dover Publications
All rights reserved. No part of this publication may be reproduced, downloaded, distributed, transmitted, or stored in any form or by any means, electronic or mechanical, without prior written from the publisher.

Dover Pocketbook Collection: Cross-Stitch Flowers is a new work, first published by Dover Publications in 2025.

ISBN-13: 978-0-486-85412-0
ISBN-10: 0-486-85412-4

Publisher: Betina Cochran
Acquisitions Editor: Allyson D'Antonio
Managing Editorial Supervisor: Susan Rattiner
Senior Production Editor: Michael Croland
Editorial, Design, and Layout: Elizabeth T. Gilbert and Coffee Cup Creative LLC
Creative Manager: Marie Zaczkiewicz
Production: Pam Weston, Tammi McKenna, Ayse Yilmaz

Printed in China
85412401   2024
www.doverpublications.com

Introduction

The art of cross-stitch has existed for thousands of years in cultures around the world. This collection of floral designs by Gerda Bengtsson has been compiled from books on the traditional art of Danish embroidery published by the Danish society Haandarbejdets Fremme (under the patronage of Her Majesty the Queen of Denmark). Haandarbejdets Fremme, known abroad as Danish Design, began in 1928 with the intention of protecting and reviving embroidery, hand-weaving, and home industries in Denmark. And now these beloved patterns are in your hands, ready to reach yet another generation.

Inside, you'll find 26 simplified charted patterns for Danish florals. Each botanical pattern features a thread palette so that you'll know the colors you'll need to complete the design. The write-in format provides a unique opportunity to create a personalized guide for future generations, ensuring that this beloved craft will not be lost but rather celebrated as it is handed down to loved ones.

This book is intended to become a family heirloom. Cherish the treasures you make with it and the connections you build along the way. Happy stitching!

Table of Contents

	PAGE
Materials	5
Prepping & Stitching	6
How to Use This Book	9
Hawthorn	10
Rose Hips	12
Brambles	14
Sloes	16
Dandelion	18
Narrow-Leaved Plantain	20
Daisy	22
Anemone	24
Black Currants	26
Bay Willow	28
Snow Gentian	30
Cowslip	32
Iceland Poppy	34
Wintergreen	36
Common Milkwort	38
Lamb's Tongue Plantain	40
Sweet Violet	42
Wood Strawberry	44
Stone Bramble	46
Crowberry	48
Cowberry	50
Cloudberry	52
Bilberry	54
Pansies	56
Cat's Foot	58
Hare's-Foot Clover	60
Complete Thread Palette	62
Carrying On the Tradition	64

Materials

Although charted designs can be used in many different forms of needlework, such as needlepoint, latch-hooking, crocheting, and knitting, the designs in this book were originally created for counted cross-stitch. Counted cross-stitch is a simple art form. The basic ingredients are a small blunt needle and a fabric that is woven evenly so it appears to be formed in regular blocks or squares.

Fabric & Tools
- A small blunt tapestry needle (ideally #24 or #26).

- Evenweave fabric. This can be linen, cotton, wool, or a blend that includes miracle fabrics. The three most popular fabrics are:

    Cotton Aida. The number of the cloth indicates the number of threads per inch; 18, 14, 11, and 8 are readily available. The higher the number, the smaller the design will appear.

    Evenweave Linen. This also comes in a variety of threads per inch. Working on evenweave linen involves a slightly different technique, which is explained on pages 7–8. Thirty-count linen will give a stitch approximately the same size as 14-count Aida.

    Hardanger Cloth. This fabric has 22 threads per inch and is available in cotton or linen.

- Embroidery thread. This can be six-strand mercerized cotton floss, crewel wool, Danish flower thread, silken and metal threads, or perle cotton. For 14-count Aida and 30-count linen, divide six-strand cotton floss and work with only two strands. For more texture, use more thread. Crewel wool is pretty on an evenweave wool fabric. Danish flower thread is a thicker thread with a matt finish; one strand equals two strands of cotton floss.

- Embroidery hoop. Use a plastic or wooden 4", 5", or 6" round or oval hoop with a screw-type tension adjuster.

- A pair of sharp embroidery scissors.

Prepping & Stitching

Prepare the fabric by whip-stitching, hemming, or zigzagging on the sewing machine to prevent the fabric from fraying at the edges. Locate the center of your chosen design; this allows you to center the design on your piece of fabric. To find the fabric's center, fold it in half both vertically and horizontally. The center stitch of the design should fall where the creases meet. It's not always convenient to begin work with the center stitch itself; it's better to start at the top of a design working horizontal rows of a single color, left to right. To locate where the top of the design should go, count squares up from the center of the design, and then count off the corresponding number of holes up from the center of the fabric. Next, place the section of the fabric to be worked tautly in the hoop. (The tighter the better, as tension makes it easier to push the needle through the holes without piercing the fabric.) Keep the screw at the top and out of the way, adjusting it to tighen as needed.

Creating the Stitches

To create a cross-stitch, push the threaded needle up through a hole in the fabric and cross over the thread intersection (or square) diagonally, left to right. This creates a half stitch (A). Now cross back, right to left, making an X.

To begin a piece, fasten the thread by holding a bit of thread on the underside of the work and anchoring it with the first few stitches (B). Create all the stitches in the same color in the same row, working left to right and slanting from bottom left to upper right (C). Then cross back, completing the Xs (D).

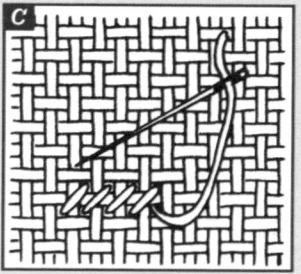

Some cross-stitchers prefer to cross each stitch as they come to it; this is fine, but be sure the slant is always in the correct direction. Of course, isolated stitches must be crossed as you work them. Vertical stitches are crossed as shown in the diagram at right (E). Holes should be used more than once; all stitches "hold hands" unless a space is indicated. Always hold the piece upright when working.

When carrying a color from one area to another, wiggle your needle under existing stitches on the underside. Do not carry a color across an open expanse of fabric for more than a few stitches as the thread will be visible from the front. To end a color, weave in and out of the underside of the stitches, perhaps making a scallop stitch or two for extra security (F). Whenever possible, end in the direction in which you are traveling, jumping up a row if necessary (G). This prevents holes caused by work being pulled in two directions. Do not make knots; they make bumps. Cut off the ends of the threads; do not leave tails because they'll show through when the work is mounted.

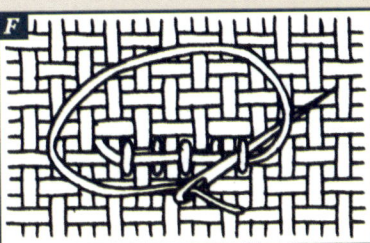

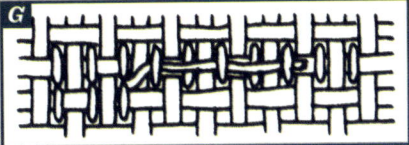

Working on Linen

Working on linen requires a slightly different technique. Evenweave linen is remarkably regular, but there are always some thin threads and some that are nubbier or fatter than others.

To even these out and to make a stitch that is easy to see, the cross-stitch is worked over two threads each way. The "square" you are covering is thus four threads (H). The first few stitches on linen are sometimes difficult, but one quickly begins "to see in twos." After the third stitch, a pattern is established, and should you inadvertently cross over three threads instead of four, the difference in slant will make the mistake immediately apparent.

Linen evenweave fabric should be worked with the selvage at the side, not at the top and bottom. Because you go over more threads, linen affords more variations in stitches (I).

The charts in this book have been simplified to include only full cross-stitches. As you gain experience, you can incoporate half stitches, three-quarter stitches (J), and backstitches (K) into your work.

Note that the finished piece of needlework will not be the same size as the charted design unless you are working on fabric that has the same number of threads per inch as the chart has squares per inch. To determine how large a finished design will be, divide the number of stitches in the design by the thread-count of the fabric. For example, if a design that is 112 stitches wide by 140 stitches deep is worked on a 14-count cloth, divide 112 stitches by 14 to get 8 and 140 by 14 to get 10; the worked design will measure 8" x 10". The same design worked on 22-count fabric would measure approximately 5" x 6 $1/2$".

Gingham or other checkered material can also be used for counted cross-stitch by making the crosses over the checks from corner to corner. To embroider a design on a fabric that does not have an evenweave, baste a lightweight Penelope canvas to the fabric. The design can then be worked from the chart by making crosses over the double mesh of the canvas. When the design is completed, remove the basting stitches and trim the edges of the Penelope canvas. The cross-stitch design will remain on the fabric.

Finishing Tips

After you have completed your stitched piece, hand wash it in cool or lukewarm water with a mild soap. Rinse well. Do not wring; instead, roll in a towel to remove excess moisture. Immediately iron on a padded surface with the needlework face down. Be sure the piece is completely dry before attempting to mount it.

To mount as a picture, center the embroidery over a pure white, rag-content mat board. Turn margins over to the back evenly. Lace the margins with button thread, top to bottom, side to side. The fabric should be tight and even, with a little tension. Never use glue for mounting. Counted cross-stitch on cotton or linen may be framed under glass.

How to Use This Book

Chart with markers every 10 blocks

Plant name

Color-coded design

Thread palette showing colors needed for project in a checklist format, plus places for color substitutions

Brief plant description

Space for writing tips, notes, and insights

See page 62 for a complete checklist of thread colors needed for the projects in this book.

Hawthorn

Crataegus

A deciduous thorny shrub or small tree, the ornamental Hawthorn yields clusters of white or pink flowers in the spring followed by small, edible pome fruits in the fall.

Thread Palette

- ◯ ■ Dark Brownish Red
- ◯ ■ Dull Blue Green
- ◯ ■ Dull Light Green
- ◯ ■ Earth Color
- ◯ ■ Fresh Red
- ◯ ■ Light Brick Red
- ◯ ■ Wine Red

Sub: _____
Sub: _____
Sub: _____

Notes:

_____
_____
_____
_____
_____
_____
_____
_____
_____
_____
_____

Tip!
These patterns have been simplified to include only full cross-stitches. Seasoned cross-stitchers may want to make the twigs thinner using half cross-stitches or backstitches.

Rose Hips

Rosa rugosa & Rosa canina

Similar to a berry, the rose hip is a fleshy, seed-containing fruit born of various rose plant species. It is generally bright red but can range from orange to dark purple. Rose hips are used medicinally in teas, powders, and oils for their anti-inflammatory properties, fatty acids, and high levels of vitamin C.

Thread Palette

- ○ Bright Red
- ○ Dull Blue Green
- ○ Dull Light Green
- ○ Earth Color
- ○ Fresh Red
- ○ Light Brick Red
- ○ Medium Green
- ○ Yellow Green

Sub: _____
Sub: _____
Sub: _____
Sub: _____

Notes:

Brambles

genus Rubus

Brambles are prickly shrubs that thrive in temperate climates. Most species produce delicious aggregate fruits, such as raspberries, blackberries, and hybrids like boysenberries.

Thread Palette

- ◯ ■ Dark Blue
- ◯ ■ Dark Yellow Green
- ◯ ■ Fresh Red
- ◯ ■ Golden Yellow
- ◯ ■ Grayish Red
- ◯ ■ Light Brick Red

- ◯ ■ Lilac
- ◯ ■ Yellow Green
- Sub: _____
- Sub: _____
- Sub: _____
- Sub: _____

Notes:

Sloes

Prunus spinosa

Also called "blackthorn," the sloe is a flowering, deciduous plant in the rose family that produces tart berries. Too sour to consume on their own, the berries (which look very much like blueberries) can be added to jams and pie fillings for a tart touch. The juice is a rich ruby pink that can act as a natural dye.

Thread Palette

- ◯ ■ Dark Blue
- ◯ ■ Golden Yellow
- ◯ ■ Gray
- ◯ ■ Lavender
- ◯ ■ Medium Green
- ◯ ■ Very Dark Brown
- ◯ ■ Yellow Green

Sub: _____
Sub: _____
Sub: _____

Notes:

Dandelion

Taraxacum officinale

A perennial plant native to Asia and Europe, the dandelion is known for its early blooming yellow flowers and fluffy seed heads. The entire plant is edible, from its peppery leaves to its nutritious roots that are used for a detoxifying tea.

Thread Palette

- ☐ ■ Brick Red
- ☐ ■ Dark Verdigris Green
- ☐ ■ Dull Light Green
- ☐ ■ Fresh Green
- ☐ ■ Light Gray

- ☐ • White
- ☐ ■ Yellow
- Sub: _____
- Sub: _____
- Sub: _____

Notes:

_____
_____
_____
_____
_____
_____
_____
_____
_____
_____
_____
_____

Narrow-Leaved Plantain

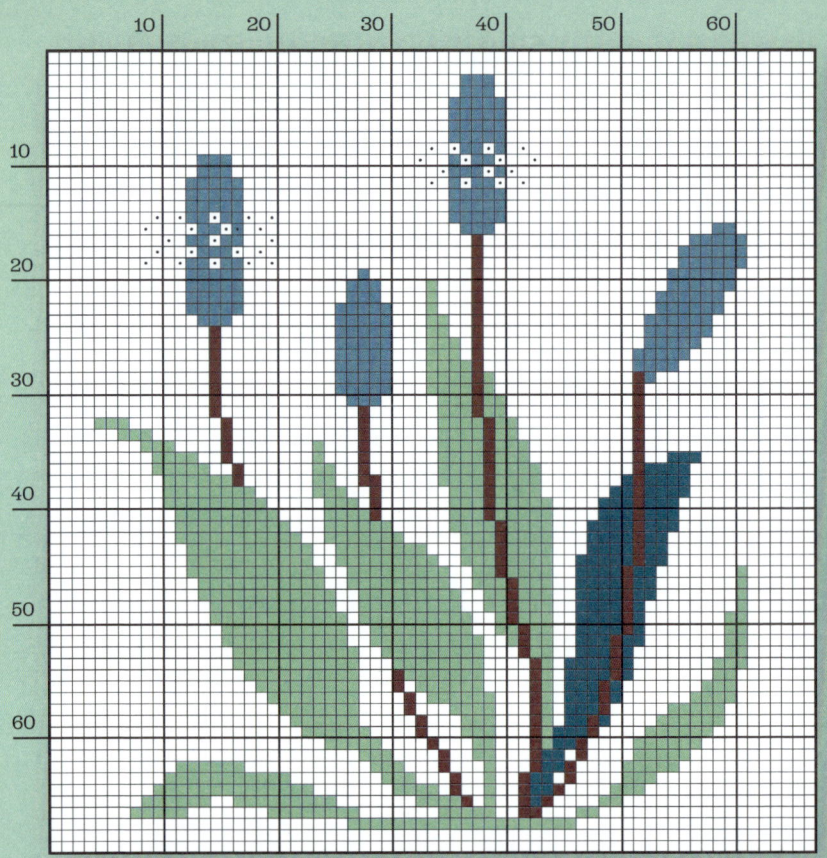

Plantago lanceolata

This flowering, edible, perennial herb features long, slender leaves that sprout from the base in a rosette formation. Despite bearing some medicinal properties, this plant is often characterized as a weed that thrives in meadows, fields, forest edges, and gardens.

Thread Palette

- ☐ ▪ Brownish Red
- ☐ ▪ Dull Blue Green
- ☐ ▪ Dull Light Green
- ☐ ▪ Verdigris Green

☐ ● White
Sub: _____
Sub: _____
Sub: _____

Notes:
_____
_____
_____
_____
_____
_____
_____
_____
_____
_____
_____
_____
_____
_____
_____
_____
_____

Daisy

Bellis perennis

A classic bontanical beauty, the daisy is a flower that features thin, white petals that fan out from a yellow disc at the center. This hardy, sun-loving flower is the national flower of the Netherlands.

Thread Palette

- ○ ■ Brick Red
- ○ ■ Dark Verdigris Green
- ○ ■ Dull Light Green
- ○ ■ Fresh Green
- ○ ■ Fresh Red
- ○ ■ Light Red
- ○ ■ White
- ○ ■ Yellow

Sub: _____
Sub: _____

Notes:

Anemone

genus Anemone

Named after the Greek word for "windflowers," anemones are perennial flowers with graceful, cupped petals and a romantic aesthetic. Their eye-catching shapes and colors make them a favorite for gardens and floral arrangements.

Thread Palette

- ◯ Brownish Rose
- ◯ Dark Green
- ◯ Earth Color
- ◯ Fresh Green
- ◯ Golden Yellow
- ◯ Grayish Red
- ◯ Medium Green
- ◯ Old Rose
- ◯ Pale Rose
- ◯ Sand Color
- ◯ Very Dark Brown
- ◯ Very Dark Green
- ◯ White
- ◯ Wine Red
- ◯ Yellow

Sub: _____
Sub: _____
Sub: _____

Notes:

Black Currants

Ribes nigrum

Black currant plants are deciduous shrubs that produce glossy, pea-sized berries. They can be pressed into juice or used in desserts, such as pies, puddings, and jams.

Thread Palette

- ○ Dark Blue
- ○ Dark Blue Violet
- ○ Dull Blue Green
- ○ Dull Light Green
- ○ Earth Color
- ○ Fresh Green
- ○ Golden Yellow
- ○ Grayish Yellow
- ○ Lavender
- ○ Light Mauve
- ○ Medium Brown
- ○ Medium Green
- ○ Very Dark Green

Sub: _____
Sub: _____
Sub: _____

Notes:

Bay Willow

Salix pentandra

This summer-blooming shrub, or small tree, is an ornamental landscape plant that features shiny, deep green leaves. Also called the laurel willow, the bay willow's fruit is a cluster of pointed capsules, and its bark is thin and ridged.

Thread Palette

- ◯ ■ Dull Blue Green
- ◯ ■ Dull Light Green
- ◯ ■ Earth Color
- ◯ ■ Fresh Green
- ◯ ■ Fresh Pale Green
- ◯ ■ Light Yellow Green
- ◯ ■ Medium Green
- ◯ ■ Very Dark Green
- ◯ ■ Yellow Green

Sub: _____
Sub: _____
Sub: _____

Notes:

Snow Gentian

Gentiana nivalis

The snow gentian—also known as "alpine gentian"—is a five-petaled, bluish-purple wildflower found in mountainous regions of the Northern Hemisphere. It is a national flower of both Austria and Switzerland.

Thread Palette

- ◯ ■ Brownish Red
- ◯ ■ Dark Cornflower
- ◯ ■ Dark Green
- ◯ ■ Dark Yellow Green
- ◯ ■ Fresh Green
- ◯ ■ Fresh Pale Green
- ◯ ■ Golden Yellow
- ◯ ■ Grayish Red
- ◯ ■ Light Cornflower
- ◯ ■ Medium Green
- ◯ • White
- ◯ ■ Yellow Green

Sub: _____
Sub: _____

Notes:
_____
_____
_____
_____
_____
_____
_____
_____
_____
_____
_____
_____
_____
_____

Cowslip

Primula veris

Also called "cowslip primrose," this fragrant yellow flower is native to Europe and western Asia. It is a perennial flower with drooping blooms that thrives in meadows, pastures, and grasslands. The cowslip is associated with fairies and the passage of souls from this world to the next.

Thread Palette

- ☐ Dark Verdigris Green
- ☐ Dull Blue Green
- ☐ Dull Light Green
- ☐ Fresh Green
- ☐ Fresh Pale Green
- ☐ Grayish Red
- ☐ Lemon Yellow
- ☐ Light Yellow Green
- ☐ Pale Light Yellow

Sub: _____
Sub: _____
Sub: _____

Notes:

_____
_____
_____
_____
_____
_____
_____
_____
_____
_____
_____
_____
_____
_____
_____

Iceland Poppy

Papaver nudicaule

The Iceland poppy has delicately frilled edges and an umbrellalike bloom that can be white, yellow, orange, red, or pink. They prefer cool summers, well-draining soil, and plenty of sun.

Thread Palette

- ☐ ■ Dark Blue Green
- ☐ ■ Dark Olive Green
- ☐ ■ Dark Verdigris Green
- ☐ ■ Dark Yellow Green
- ☐ ■ Dull Light Green
- ☐ ■ Earth Color
- ☐ ■ Golden Yellow
- ☐ ■ Lemon Yellow
- ☐ ■ Pale Verdigris Green
- ☐ ■ Verdigris Green
- ☐ ■ Yellow Green

Sub: _____
Sub: _____
Sub: _____

Notes:

Wintergreen

genus Gaultheria

Wintergreen has rounded, rich green leaves that emit a mild minty fragrance. It blooms with clusters of small, bell-shaped flowers that can be white or pink. In early winter, it grows bright red berries.

Thread Palette

- ○ ■ Brownish Red
- ○ ■ Dark Green
- ○ ■ Dull Light Green
- ○ ■ Fresh Bluish Red
- ○ ■ Fresh Green
- ○ ■ Golden Yellow
- ○ ■ Grayish Red
- ○ ■ Medium Brown
- ○ ■ Medium Green
- ○ ■ Old Rose
- ○ ■ Pale Rose

Sub: _____
Sub: _____
Sub: _____

Notes:
_____
_____
_____
_____
_____
_____
_____
_____
_____
_____
_____
_____
_____

Common Milkwort

Polygala vulgaris

This perennial beauty thrives in a range of habitats across the Northern Hemisphere, from grasslands and mountains to sandy seasides. It has blue, purple, or white flowers and slender, alternating leaves.

Thread Palette

- ○ ■ Dull Blue Green
- ○ ■ Fresh Green
- ○ ■ Fresh Pale Green
- ○ ■ Lavender
- ○ ■ Light Blue
- ○ ■ Light Cornflower
- ○ ■ Light Mauve
- ○ ■ Medium Green

Sub: _____
Sub: _____

Notes:

Lamb's Tongue Plantain

Plantago lanceolata

This perennial plant goes by a number of names, including ribwort plantain and narrow-leaved plantain (see page 20). It features slender, edible leaves with long, parallel grooves. Its brown flowers are located on a dense spike that sits atop a tall stem.

Thread Palette

- ○ ■ Brick Red
- ○ ■ Dark Green
- ○ ■ Dark Olive Green
- ○ ■ Dull Light Green
- ○ ■ Fresh Green
- ○ ■ Fresh Pale Green
- ○ ■ Grayish Yellow
- ○ ■ Medium Green
- ○ ■ Pale Rose

Sub: _____
Sub: _____
Sub: _____

Notes:

Sweet Violet

Viola odorata

This perennial blooms with bluish-purple flowers that emanate with a perfume-like aroma. It's no wonder that this beloved plant, with its heart-shaped leaves, has become a symbol for love, innocence, and loyalty.

Thread Palette

- ☐ ■ Dark Green
- ☐ ■ Dull Light Green
- ☐ ■ Fresh Green
- ☐ ■ Grayish Red
- ☐ ■ Light Mauve
- ☐ ■ Lilac
- ☐ ■ Medium Green
- ☐ ■ Orange Yellow

Sub: _____
Sub: _____

Notes:

Wood Strawberry

Fragaria vesca

Also called "wild strawberry" and "woodland strawberry," this perennial plant produces small, sweet, juicy red fruit. It is a groundcover plant related to the rose family that blooms with five-petaled white flowers in spring and summer.

Thread Palette

- ◯ ▇ Carrot Color
- ◯ ▇ Dull Light Green
- ◯ ▇ Earth Color
- ◯ ▇ Fresh Green
- ◯ ▇ Fresh Red
- ◯ ▇ Golden Yellow
- ◯ ▇ Grayish Red
- ◯ ▇ Medium Green
- ◯ ▇ Very Dark Green
- ◯ ▇ Warm Peach

Sub: _____
Sub: _____

Notes:

Stone Bramble

Rubus saxatilis

The most common bramble species in northern Europe, the stone bramble glows with shiny, bright red berries. This shrub grows well in dry, stony ground, hence the name.

Thread Palette

- ☐ ■ Bright Red
- ☐ ■ Dark Green
- ☐ ■ Dark Yellow Green
- ☐ ■ Dull Light Green
- ☐ ■ Earth Color
- ☐ ■ Fresh Green
- ☐ ■ Fresh Red
- ☐ ■ Golden Yellow
- ☐ ■ Light Brick Red
- ☐ ■ Medium Green
- ☐ ■ Verdigris Green

Sub: _____
Sub: _____
Sub: _____

Notes:

Crowberry

Empetrum nigrum

Present throughout the Northern Hemisphere, the crowberry is a low evergreen shrub in the heather family. It produces pink flowers followed by dark-colored fruits that can be used to make wine, liqueur, jellies, and jams.

Thread Palette

- ○ ■ Black
- ○ ■ Dark Blue
- ○ ■ Dark Green
- ○ ■ Earth Color
- ○ ■ Fresh Green
- ○ ■ Fresh Pale Green
- ○ ■ Golden Yellow
- ○ ■ Light Blue
- ○ ■ Medium Brown

Sub: _____
Sub: _____
Sub: _____

Notes:

Cowberry

Vaccinium vitis-idaea

Known as lingonberry in Sweden, this evergreen shrub can withstand very cold temperatures. It produces small, ruby-red berries that can be sugared and cooked into compotes and jams.

Thread Palette

- ◯ ▨ Carrot Color
- ◯ ▨ Dark Green
- ◯ ▨ Dark Yellow Green
- ◯ ▨ Dull Light Green
- ◯ ▨ Earth Color
- ◯ ▨ Fresh Green
- ◯ ▨ Fresh Red
- ◯ ▨ Light Brick Red
- ◯ ▨ Medium Green
- ◯ ▨ Very Dark Green
- ◯ ▨ Wine Red

Sub: _____
Sub: _____
Sub: _____

Notes:

Cloudberry

Rubus chamaemorus

The cloudberry is a low-growing herbaceous plant native to bog habitats of the Arctic and subarctic. It has charming five-lobed leaves and blooms with white flowers. Considered a delicacy, the juicy berries are yellow to orange in color and resemble a blackberry in shape.

Thread Palette

- ◯ ▪ Carrot Color
- ◯ ▪ Dark Green
- ◯ ▪ Dark Yellow Green
- ◯ ▪ Fresh Green
- ◯ ▪ Fresh Pale Green
- ◯ ▪ Fresh Red
- ◯ ▪ Grayish Red
- ◯ ▪ Orange Yellow
- ◯ ▪ Pale Light Yellow
- ◯ ▪ Wine Red

Sub: _____
Sub: _____
Sub: _____
Sub: _____

Notes:

Bilberry

Vaccinium myrtillus

Also known as "European blueberry" and "whortleberry," this deciduous shrub produces sweet, nutritious berries commonly used in desserts. In autumn, its leaves turn a vibrant red.

Thread Palette

- ◯ ■ Bluish Red
- ◯ ■ Dull Blue Green
- ◯ ■ Earth Color
- ◯ ■ Fresh Bluish Red
- ◯ ■ Fresh Green
- ◯ ■ Fresh Pale Green
- ◯ ■ Gray
- ◯ ■ Lavender
- ◯ ■ Light Yellow Green

Sub: _____
Sub: _____
Sub: _____

Notes:

Pansies

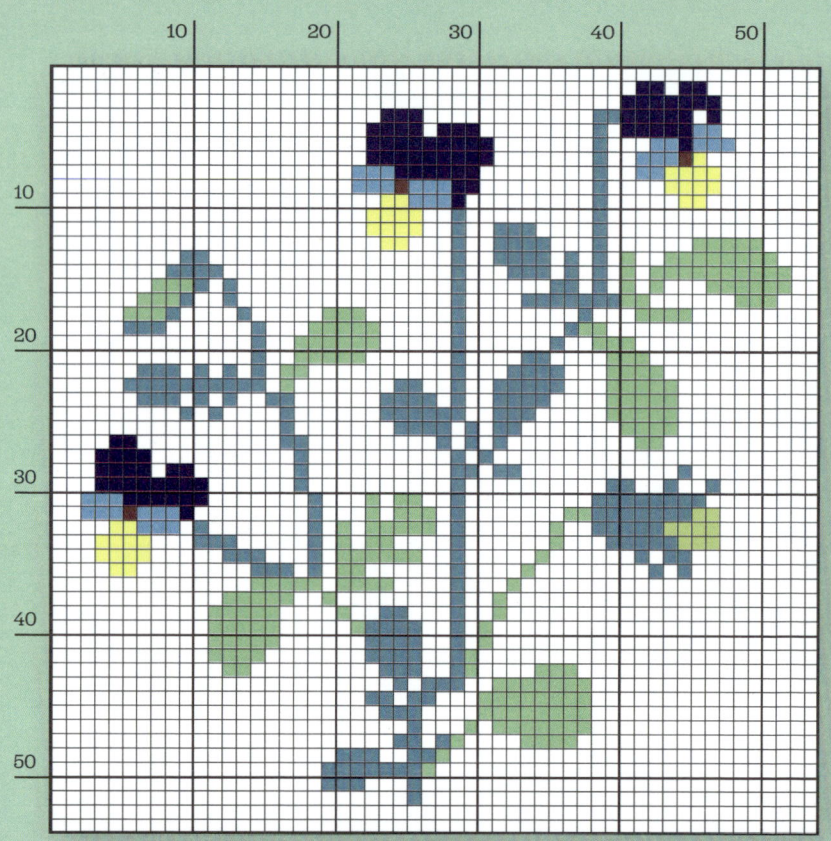

Viola tricolor

A relative of the violet, the wild pansy is generally purple, blue, white, and yellow. The flower symbolizes thoughts, likely related to its pensive, facelike markings. The pansy's petals are arranged in a distinct formation: four petals face up, and one petal faces down.

Thread Palette

- ◯ ▉ Dull Blue Green
- ◯ ▉ Dull Light Green
- ◯ ▉ Lemon Yellow
- ◯ ▉ Light Blue
- ◯ ▉ Light Yellow Green
- ◯ ▉ Navy Blue
- ◯ ▉ Very Dark Brown

Sub: _____
Sub: _____
Sub: _____

Notes:

Cat's Foot

Antennaria dioica

Also called "pussytoes" and "mountain everlasting," this perennial plant is a flowering herb found in the Northern Hemisphere. It has silvery green leaves and clusters of pink flowers that look like a cat's paw.

Thread Palette

- ◯ ■ Bluish Red
- ◯ ■ Dark Verdigris Green
- ◯ ■ Dull Light Green
- ◯ ■ Earth Color
- ◯ ■ Fresh Green
- ◯ ■ Light Brick Red
- ◯ ■ Medium Brown
- ◯ ■ Medium Green
- ◯ ■ Verdigris Green
- ◯ ● White

Sub: _____

Sub: _____

Notes:

Hare's-Foot Clover

Trifolium arvense

This European native of the legume family is known for its distinct fuzzy flower head that resembles a rabbit's foot. The pink flowers with silky hairs sit atop perky stems with petite leaflets. Another name for this plant is "stone clover," referring to its preference for sandy soils.

Thread Palette

- ◯ ■ Dull Blue Green
- ◯ ■ Dull Light Green
- ◯ ■ Fresh Green
- ◯ ■ Gray
- ◯ ■ Light Gray
- ◯ ■ Medium Green
- ◯ ■ Old Rose
- ◯ ■ Pale Rose

Sub: _____

Sub: _____

Notes:

Complete Thread Palette

- ○ ■ Black
- ○ ■ Bluish Red
- ○ ■ Brick Red
- ○ ■ Bright Red
- ○ ■ Brownish Red
- ○ ■ Brownish Rose
- ○ ■ Carrot Color
- ○ ■ Dark Blue
- ○ ■ Dark Blue Green
- ○ ■ Dark Blue Violet
- ○ ■ Dark Brownish Red
- ○ ■ Dark Cornflower
- ○ ■ Dark Green
- ○ ■ Dark Olive Green
- ○ ■ Dark Verdigris Green
- ○ ■ Dark Yellow Green
- ○ ■ Dull Blue Green
- ○ ■ Dull Light Green
- ○ ■ Earth Color
- ○ ■ Fresh Bluish Red
- ○ ■ Fresh Green
- ○ ■ Fresh Pale Green
- ○ ■ Fresh Red
- ○ ■ Golden Yellow
- ○ ■ Gray
- ○ ■ Grayish Red
- ○ ■ Grayish Yellow

- ○ ■ Lavender
- ○ ■ Lemon Yellow
- ○ ■ Light Blue
- ○ ■ Light Brick Red
- ○ ■ Light Cornflower
- ○ ■ Light Gray
- ○ ■ Light Mauve
- ○ ■ Light Red
- ○ ■ Light Yellow Green
- ○ ■ Lilac
- ○ ■ Medium Brown
- ○ ■ Medium Green
- ○ ■ Navy Blue
- ○ ■ Old Rose
- ○ ■ Orange Yellow
- ○ ■ Pale Light Yellow
- ○ ■ Pale Rose
- ○ ■ Pale Verdigris Green
- ○ ■ Sand Color
- ○ ■ Verdigris Green
- ○ ■ Very Dark Brown
- ○ ■ Very Dark Green
- ○ ■ Warm Peach
- ⊙ ■ White
- ○ ■ Wine Red
- ○ ■ Yellow
- ○ ■ Yellow Green

Favorite Thread Brands

Favorite Color Combinations

Substitutions & Equivalents

Carrying On the Tradition

Personal Message: